for Andrew & Emily

Late Snow and Hellebore

with best wishes —
Melinda ☺

Late Snow and Hellebore

Poems by

Melinda Rizzo

Cover design by Shay Culligan

ISBN: 978-1-950462-58-2

Kelsay Books Inc.

kelsaybooks.com

502 S 1040 E, A119
American Fork, Utah 84003

For Dad—who inspired my lifelong love affair with soil,
never dirt, and with seeds, rusted red wagons,
short handled spades, hoes, rakes and compost.

And for Phil and Adam—thanks for giving me garden space,
in every way, for the tending.

Acknowledgments

There are so many, many people, places and things that impact a poet's work and life—from Aunt Terry who called me *Poet* as a child to favorite poems and poets. To artists and musicians, thank you. To cooks and gardeners—an everlasting thank you and amen.

This book could not have been be possible without the steadfast, constant support, sometime needling and always encouragement of fierce fellow FOUR poets and friends: Patricia Goodrich, Geriann McLaughlin and Cleveland Wall, thanks women you mean the world to me.

Pat you hold my feet to the fire. Geriann your thoughtful insights are true to the mark. Cleveland, you challenge me to do my <u>best</u> work, with grit or elegance.

To Laura MacPherson whose recent support and encouragement helped me down the home stretch, thank you.

To the Very Reverend Anthony R. "Tony" Pompa, many thanks for a holy space to share my work through spoken and printed word at regular Cathedral Church of the Nativity Celtic Spirit services.

To Dr. Christopher Bursk, your workshops at Bucks County Community College in Newtown, Pennsylvania enrich, challenge, inspire and *encourage* those who attend them. You help us be our best selves. I owe a huge debt to Chris for the formation of this book—without his patience, honesty, guidance and support, it would not have been possible.

In thanksgiving for these publications and spoken word venues, online and in print for publishing and offering my work a bigger voice: Poetry 24, Petoskey Stone Press, Cathedral Church of the Nativity, Unitarian Universalist Church of the Lehigh Valley and Quakertown Alive!, Autumn Alive! Festival and 2019 Bucks County Poet Laureate contest.

Contents

III Artichoke—a thistle, the globe or French artichoke
    consumed before buds bloom

I

Late Snow—Tribe of Helleborae
and belonging

Culinaria Interpretata

It begins with blackberries.
Luscious, plum-colored, nubby and nested
in boxes at the farmers market.

I am their instrument,
the way wind from lungs fills an oboe reed
creating A flat, or B, or C sharpness.

I offer translations: round and plump folded into
chocolate sponge roll filling with freshly whipped cream,
blackberries, scattered adornment, hold sway.

I join together raspberries, butter, sugar and eggs—
filling for a sweet tart, crowned with
chunky crumbs of flour, unsalted butter

alongside sugar—white as stardust
the secret ingredient…
sssssssshhhhhhh…cold tap water.

It all comes down to this.
Water drizzled coarse crumbs,
now bound like family photographs.

When I sat with my father, dying
his eyes glazed, unknowable
until the nurse startled him.

Your daughter's here,
and your grandson.
She smiled at me, said

you have to shout,
and left the room.
My voice becomes a runner,

chasing my father
for the last time.
And I'm not ready:

not ready for this departure,
not ready for the blackberries
to go out of season

or the perennial, everlasting loss
the last slice represents,
a moment's notice before it is consumed.

Ravens

I push everything I know off to the side.
For a moment I watch these two predators,
fiddling and flapping, bracing on thick branches; letting go

in the stiffening foliage of my ash tree.
It's November. They are black as Syrian oil.
I listen to their dialog. *Caw* resonates deep in the gullet.

Like the ruffle of shuffling playing cards, it starts slow,
punctuated by the final fan-slap as the last card folds
the deck, next quiet roulette of dealer's hands.

I imagine what they might've said: Passion,
a bargain? Scolding or rolled eyes over chores,
divvying seed? Who was wrong…who was right?

Caw is the end of a sentence.
I do not speak Bird, but in this
aging moment, I wish I did.

One to the other over the fussing
and how significant or not,
it would all mean in the end.

I wonder if I could learn Raven,
a dialect of Bird, one of thousands,
perhaps, tens or hundreds of thousands.
No. Millions. And if I could begin—
even just begin; nothing more for now.
To understand…what new worlds?

Rocks

Burning rock bereft of blood,
bone, tendon and sinew
litters the nearby woodlands—

a silent rock concert.
Today the rocks are dry, straight through.
American Revolution-era stone barn

chafes from a new, wood-frame addition.
Massive man-barn sits skewed, out of place.
The framing a woman, maybe, or

prodigal son trying to know his father.
It is skinned—off to the side.
I could sit still, perched

on one of these crystalline
metamorphic rocks, composed
of dark gneiss and diabase.

Two million years or more of knowing,
of listening to wind sail through chinks
in mortar, through handicraft stone pointing.

Wait for the steaming cup of coffee
that won't come unless I make it and
pour it streaming from the carafe.

I'll sit awhile, listening,
waiting and listening
for a long time.

Color of Sound

For Vincent van Gogh

I waited for a sound and stumbled over
syllables, long vowels, consonants
strung together, twelve oyster pearls

becoming a word.
And the word became a new sound,
not like the parts of its sum at all.

Something new, like my corn spoonbread.
Garlic, melted butter, extra sharp English cheddar—
the color of tangelos, milk, meal and eggs.

The swish of wire whisk, tensioned scratch
of metal against ceramic, swirling egg yolks alone.
These beaten are transformed, color of sunshine.

Next, I'll add stone ground cornmeal
the yolks become part of a gritty mush,
yellow as van Gogh's sunflowers in St. Remy

and his solitary, yellow room
because everyone said he was crazy
and painted in open fields.

Did he get depressed and paint
some more, cut off his ear; paint some more,
scream, tear his tortured clothes,

paint some more, and more?
What was he searching for?
A good egg?

And when he found himself
in a straw-colored wheat field
with the sound of crows and their airy

feathered wings lifting in fright
and the repelling echo of the gunshot ending him—
what was the color of sound?

My uncle used a shotgun,
braced it against a makeshift fence,
to keep the few livestock in and

trigger tied with twine. The sound
of their bodies—van Gogh's and my uncle's
as they smacked the hard earth—

a half century apart, and still the same.

The sound of the wheat as it brushed
van Gogh's smock and trousers going down
and him going down, and crows going up.

Did they shepherd his spirit, freed?
I must believe that. And was there a sound
out of that yellow despair and his suffering

his yellows mirror my field—
the color of cornmeal spoonbread
and August sunflowers

in my garden patch, as I gather them,
cut them from thick hollow stalks,
singe their wounds charred by orange flame.

Dear Mom,

For years, I'd look for mother substitutes—
under rocks, in closets, on the Ferris wheel in July at the shore.
Eventually, like hand recoiling from a hot stove burner, I stopped.

At about 15 I realized I didn't really know what
I was looking for anyway—and the fresh sting of raw burn
slowly began to glaze over, reduced to a dull haphazard ache.

Losing a parent—and I've
been zero for two for a long time now—
it's like a reverse birth: You are never the same.

Spring's late this year.
The lilac blossoms are still, small, and tight.
They clutch to themselves in cool mornings.

A clump of wild violets—I never planted these—
shimmer in dappled sunlight. They're seated
up against the fence, fully fledged.

These little ones must receive
some adopted warmth from painted wood,
some sheltering protection from season's ebb and flow.

I lost you at 11, learned comfort
in familiar, daily routine: Brushing my teeth,
Grammy's "silver dollar" pancake breakfasts.

You were born on May Day, 100 years ago today,
and on May Day still, the United Kingdom celebrates.
Roman Goddess Flora is feted and rejoices.

Girls wear fresh garlands, have twirled around the
Maypole, for 2,000 years or longer! Everyone gets a bank
holiday, a return on investment they can count.

Yearly, I promise myself I'll make a May basket
to hang on my front doorknob. Redolent with spring flowers
from my garden and lavender sateen ribbons.

I would do it this year, *truly,* I would,
except the daffodils are spent. Delighted violets,
too small, to peep out from the rim,

and the lilacs—your blessed favorites—aren't ready.

Love-
Melinda
PS-

Pear blossoms and pine, bursting hyacinth
and a painted maple basket. Among reluctant,
white lilac blossoms, I find my courage.

An Ode to Sons

For Adam

I

How could Daedalus have known in Sicily
betrayal would fill his mouth. The ant
and a silken thread winding through the

trap set by King Minos and his smooth conch shell,
inner shrine and pearled protection, sacred spirit habitation.
Was the amber honey tempting the ant forward, simple

sweetness: Daedalus, and his cleverness ensnared?
After all Sicily embraced the architect—its people
longed for indoor baths and running water.

The wondrous palace rises up, leading Minos
to his revenge. A father's heart is fragile,
after all, and Minotaur lay dead.

II

My son brings me a fist of dandelions.
Stems thread through his slender toddler fingers.
He demands we put them in water.

I fetch a vacant shot glass, he stubs stems into it.
Icaras flew too close to the sun, ignored
the liquid fire running down his arms, the wet burn,

his humanity, unable to support the blast
from Helios' breath. The feathers came
undone, and Icaras drowned.

III

In the evenings I bathe my son.
Scrub his fragile back, hollow scoop of his neck.
Slather soap and work a soft baby washcloth

between the creases of his toes.
He emerges clean and whole and safe
leaving water and suds.

I shake off bedtime chill, as we leave fairytales,
fabled warnings and the Greeks, behind.

Mirror Tricks

I take down the bathroom mirror,
hold it cockeyed, turn myself,
check the jean's waistband,

or line of sweater, fall of fabric from hips,
flush of velvet across my calves,
sway of an A-line skirt.

Settled back on its Snow White, "mirror,
mirror" perch above the pedestal sink,
I check beginning lines etching

signature along the corners of my eyes,
but no, they're my mother's blue eyes
and everyone said so.

"Why darling, you have your mother's eyes,"
and as a kid I'd marvel, *"How about that!"*
All this because I'm going out,

and I don't have a full length mirror.
I make do....don't we all?
Earlier today, I watched my young son

help another child at the playground.
A generous spirit reflected in his eyes,
as they played on swings together.

My eyes passed down,
my mother's eyes transfigured.

Alphabet 1

Does the A represent anything more
than the sounds it makes
combined with another vowel

or how A sounds long
with an e jabbed on the end.
The symbol of a phonetic system

having evolved over thousands of years
to arrive at A next to B and then
the C in Cain?

We're not told if, or even how,
Adam and Eve mourned their son,
Abel, bleeding to death

from his brother's hand.
Simply that they had another son:
His name much farther down

in the alphabet's lineage: Seth.
Nor are we told if Cain was dressed down,
if Adam was driven to *so much grief,*

to relentless despair, that he slammed himself
into the dust he knew so well.
Did the first sacred ashes come from this?

We're told simply the brutal mark of murder
would be too much—too much even,
for Cain to bear.

Muguet

Mary's tears, *May Day in France*

In Menerbes, a hilltown village carved
against the Luberon Mountains, Adam
played with some French children.
They never spoke but laughed and took turns

on the swings, pumping legs faster and higher,
and chains squeaked like any back home,
because play doesn't really need any
translation, and a smile is universal.

So I smile at the man next to me.
I ask him what they mean,
the *Lily of the Valley,*
or Muguet in French.

He tells me Muguet, it is tradition
to share them on French Labor Day,
May 1, my mother's birthday.
He does not explain about the flowers.

We are in a Parisian airport.
Two flight attendants walk past,
crisp in their slender high heals
and seamless nude stockings.

The ladies continue arm-in-arm,
into the sunshine, holding
dainty Muguet bouquets—fringed,
silent bells, trailing small luggage cases.

The French celebrate language
Voltaire, Degas, French
Revolution, crepes, madeleines,
and one another on May 1.

And now I am desperate for *Muguet,*
packed in little pots, or tied
with silky ribbons around
a clutch of tender stems.

Stains

The blackberries glisten in my father's hands,
fingertips turned to dusk in the twilight.
The blackberries are a bonus,

sweet reminder of lazy late
June and berry picking.
During this ripening season,

I miss him most. I blanch Jersey peaches,
stir them together with blackberry
brandy and Mexican vanilla.

Whisk flour and granular sugar,
baking powder, salt and whole milk
thin batter poured over peach quarters

and melted, sweet cream butter.
I broadcast the blackberries
across the silken batter,

like a farmer sowing seed by hand,
at the end of a warm June afternoon, palms
filled and scattered, full of fruit and memory.

Dear Dad,

For November 7, 2018

They're playing *Moon River* on the radio.
Not the Andy Williams version, the
instrumental, one of your favorites.

I made myself a soft-boiled egg
and got it right! White just set,
summer sunshine yolk all ooze runny-

and I did soft white bread toast to dip it,
it wasn't Wonder, but it was wonderful—
with the crust a little crisp shattered snap.

This year you'd have been 100
your odometer silence, and mine
running toward 57 in December.

A year longer than Mom got to be—
So on November 7, 2018,
I'll head to Philadelphia.

On your birthday I'll order a Manhattan, straight up,
with two maraschino cherries on a pick,
and I'll give it a swirl….

I remember now why the eggs matter-
in your two-room walk up at 5th and Girard
Mom made you custardy soft-boiled eggs,

she told me so—with Wonder Bread toast.
She'd use the traffic light on the corner
as perfect three-minute timer.

Love-
PS-
It's late September.

I sit in the evening shade,
pony bottle of Rolling Rock in one hand
and farmer's field at my feet.

I listen to the corn gossip as sun fades
while Mandarin moon, *as wide as your smile*
climbs the horizon.

Meals

I look for Communion in lemon roasted chicken
dressed with woody fresh rosemary.
In beef bolar pot roast surrounded by Idaho potatoes

and thick planks of carrots cut on the slant.
Yesterday I peeled white potatoes to settle myself,
considered the tapas meal I'd be making:

Vanilla Pastel Tres Leches, Nicaraguan
three milks cake soaked with canned and whole milk,
mounded with freshly whipped cream.

Tres Leches cake for three women, and
my first Mexican mole. I bought
luxuriant chipotle chili powder,

rusted Aztec dust
and Perugia's darkest chocolate.
I'm fusing the world through a sauté pan.

I'm galvanizing generations with sugar,
flour, salt and eggs.
I'm offering up my heart, expectant,

arranged and piping hot on a crisp, linen-white platter.

Sunday

The house is empty save for me, the Vince Guaraldi Trio
and George Winston's piano invocation: *December*.

Yesterday I watched bare maples, their heavy boughs
bulge, sway and lift a chorus of settling gray rock doves.

The sun burned patches in the snow, and filled tractor ruts.
They brace cornfields and fallows, expose weary grass

and Gaia's frozen skin. I am not wintering, no—not yet,
surely past late summer's heat and steam,

its frivolity. We take turns—trinity of father, son, and mother.
We haul split, brittle oak, ash and sycamore from

old wood shed to back door. Our grip fraught
with ice and stubble gingerly stepped, footing unsure.

The wheelbarrow employs ruts in day-old snow,
grooving path, arrow straight, ruts steady

both handler and cargo. An old adage reminds me,
wood heats thrice: Cutting to gathering in,

split and stack; and last the comfortable burn.

I have a year to stand watch until we sit by December
again, distance greater than wheeling a barrow of wood.

I'll Never Curse the Snow

For Roy

For six months he didn't look sick.
Not unless you knew him; looked close.
Noticed the slack hammocks at his neck

droop of his chest, sadness of limbs.
The slow swelling where his spleen
was growing inside his belly—we couldn't see.

Even still, he was game.
Greeted each new day selflessly, regal head,
rich chestnut eyes and lashing, feathered tail.

That year we traversed December's frozen fields,
tucked under a thick snow cap.
Roy freely walked for miles.

When ice storms came and the
white pine, Norway and blue spruce sagged,
weighted down from hours of storming

I'd strap Black Diamond crampons
over my boots—walk some more, marvel
at left-over corn, Popsicle coated, glistening.

We'd trek nature trails, spook deer,
his knowing gaze tuned to a twig snap,
he'd source all sounds beyond my hearing

and when the black sky was salted with stars,
we'd watch red foxes, shrill and jump
against the sweep of white in the tree line beyond fields.

Constant ash and silver maple line the foot path
back and forth to the house. What a wintering we had!
Hundreds, no thousands of passes, a rhythm familiar.

He gave me more, and more and more,
so I'll never see winter the same way,
and I'll never curse the snow.

After the Benediction

When do we stop being angry
with the dead for leaving us?
As if it were an option and their choice:

Hmmm…shall I stay here,
where April rain spatters skin
or move inside to a warm kitchen

and hot oil leaping up from a skillet
as a thick rib-eye lands in cast iron,
an incense smoke offering. *Shall I stay*

for the taste of boiled corn slaked from the cob,
golden buttered egg noodles, or
smooth, fragrant raspberry puree,

Relish birthdays and chocolate cake
with creamy fudge frosting, straight
from the Hershey's tin recipe.

Dad you'd have enjoyed coffee
with light cream paired with a slice
of fresh blueberry pie at my table.

Mother my chock-a-block brimmed
carrot cake, double loaded with currents,
clove scented, would have rested scant,

luscious moments on your tongue.
Grammy, the tang of crème fraiche
over fresh, fat blackberries—July's delight

coupled with tiny glasses of sweet wine.
The ritual mix, push and roll of sugar
cookie cut-outs—*just you and me*—

and the smells from a satisfied oven.

I'm letting you all off the hook…I believe
you'd have stayed, if given half a chance.

Transposed Tenor

For Adolphe Sax, inventor of the saxophone, patent 1846

Imagine dissolving
into a single breath.
The slick slip-slide journey

through embouchured lip
taut facial muscle, tongue and teeth
holding all in place,

the collective tightens on slim reed,
cold brass, held by ligature
diaphragm gathers and is braced

to push the swell, like birthing. Your
whole self and everything you know,
become a moment's single note:

B flat or open C major—
whole, half or graced.
Timing doesn't matter.

There's a host of transposed tenor
saxophone literature to ruminate over,
abundant treble clef notes to choose.

Birth to death, start and finish,
dates on a gravestone
separated by a dash, a lifetime.

You're a note born beyond the bell.

Burned

The man in Ireland was found burned to ashes
before his fireplace, embers smoldering.
West Galway Coroner Dr Ciaran McLoughlin's verdict:

Spontaneous Combustion -
when a human body burns
without external accelerant.

We burn from love, from lust.
We burn in August beside
the oceans lapping tide.

My father used to get burned up,
when I'd done something to piss him off,
or someone else had: Like stopping short

on the Freeway, or the time at the Acme,
when I was seven, awkwardly teetering and
steering the shopping cart and by accident

drove it up the back of his heels.
I've burned bacon to wood in a sweaty
iron frying pan, burned walnuts in the oven,

to charred pebbles beyond use,
beyond recognition, too late to
rescue them. I've torched bridges, too.

Garden Psalm

The remains of my garden wait.
Their music has played out.
Now reedy stalks and brittle stems

perhaps an Andes goddess
could make music from these. Empty
butternut squash now percussive shaker,

forgotten orphan from the harvest,
with seeds solid and silent inside its hips,
the sound of woodpeckers

nearby, tat-a-tating on a tree,
I'll survey for insects in April.
Mildew creeps along zinnia leaf rims,

softening una corda on
a three-pedal grand piano
before sustain and *Clair de Lune*.

Late September is coy,
waves to November from afar.
Choral strains and December's

carols ring silver threads across my garden.
The Coventry Carol's lamentation.
Hark the Herald Angels Sing jubilation,

hushed and reverential *Silent Night*.

January's Epiphany found faded in
purpled frozen kale and
potted parsley drooped, flat.

Stubborn finches knock a seed or two from
leftover Chianti and Lemon Zest sunflowers,
their beaks staccato eighth notes.

All simmering under the soil,
like an orchestra poised before the first note.
I wait for the conductor's baton to begin anew.

The Promise of Artichokes

Two sassy artichokes simmer in dry white wine,
sliced lemon, coarse Parisian saltiness and
cracked peppercorns: white, red and dusky black.

I picked lovage *Levisticum officinaleas,* a stand in
because the lemon thyme didn't overwinter.
Chives as resurrection, small and new.

I'll simmer mild yellow onions in olive oil,
pound buttery garlic croutons to coarse crumbs,
press minced fresh garlic, pungent and rich, into the mix.

Mellowed with heat and flame, I'll toss the sauté
with grated Romano, ancient conqueror
greedy for expansion, as Rome conquered

Helvetii Swiss pasture, and water in plenty.
I'll scoop out thorny choke—cloak
and dagger cunning. If swallowed it is capable of

snuffing its victim's breath, forced subjugation.
I'll replace its missing heart with
softened onion and cheeses, intermingled,

delectable on the tongue, press more filling
between pliant, yielding leaves.
I've become practiced at fresh artichokes,

no longer afraid.

Ase dies alone on the mountain

From Peer Gynt, Edward Grieg

Peer Gynt drives imaginary reindeer
to a castle of pretense, takes his mother Ase
along for a fairy-tale joyride to heaven.

Peer narrates the sky,
the stars, the pearly gates.
Ibsen wrote a five act poem,

with trolls, peasants, brides and
blacksmiths, kings and cooks,
braggarts, lies and redemption

gathered in one piece for the stage.
Afterward he commissioned
Grieg for incidental music.

In *Ase's Death Song* the strings
create her mountains, crags and valleys,
her longing and sadness, these become ours—

taut from hanging on,
bound and released
in emptied mother love.

Two Norwegians, their lives
buttressed by the North Sea.
Was Ase searching for a castle

and for rest made from pure, radiant light?
Pillars of light piercing the sky,
a roof framed and shingled with light.

Illuminating walls, studs, even
fastening screws and nails,
all made from pure light?

On the Last Day

for Diana Weiss

And the head of a pin will be crowded with angels
in black leather boots tied at their ankles.

What more is there? Angels are not nuns
though the habit may be a decision.

Postulates offering their lives, becoming
the question before it's been asked.

And the wimple, a flying feast
covering crowning glory,

perhaps shielding a head shorn clean.
Simpler hygiene: no shampoo

no curlers, no blow drying,
no gray-haired wrestling matches.

What's simpler than no hair at all??
Back to the pin and all those ankles -

tapping to Coltrane, or Gillespie,
jamming over Miles Davis, leather

toes testing, how far the edge extends.

List

Palm of sunshine pressed to neck's nape
in rising, February morning's chill.

Lima bean seed, hard stub dropped
into crumbled, fresh tilled loam.

Scent of chocolate cake, first cut and slice.
Olive oil sizzled in a cast iron skillet.

Spanish onion and shallot's rasp,
first lyric puff from a Jazz saxophone.

Bourbon Manhattan's maiden journey, initiating burn
wrapped around the back of a 21-year-old throat.

Sweet and piquant salty spray, ocean's ardent
wave rides at the Jersey shore in August.

Poached eggs laid down over slabs of French
toasted sourdough, cracked pepper dusted—for spice.

Staccato cry of life, newborn from the womb,
soft squirm of premature baby's journey to the breast.

Orphaned regret after death takes a mother,
a father, a favorite uncle, aunt; a childhood friend.

Forgiveness offered, before the ask.

II

Hellebore—or *Lenten Rose* blooms early, from
Helle *to injure,* and bora *food*

Mid winter Garden

It takes a Lenten wilderness to plot the rows.
The weather's been mild this season, and
I could till out a patch with ease.

Perhaps I'll sow early spring leeks,
a reminder of St. David's Day and
my Welsh great-grandmother, *Abbie-Melinda,*

or a nod to Henry V—a Welshman, too,
wearing a leek to battle in
my favorite Shakespearean history.

I'd be reminded as I hill the rows
of how St. David's sermon on a grassy slope,
became miracle, while the earth beneath him thrummed.

Soil gathering itself, it rose up
cresting to the astonishment,
I imagine, of the now elevated St. David.

This year March the first unites
St. David's death-day,
 and Ash Wednesday, as one.

I think I'll hunt for leek seed.
Gardening lifts me a little closer to heaven.

Day 1

The cross wears a purple shroud,
centered on the altar
of The Good Shepherd Chapel.

A baby grouses in his mother's lap,
noisily slurps breakfast in the last row
of tight knit chairs and faithful kneelers.

I walk to my car, forehead
smudged with burnt palms,
and last year's jubilant celebrations.

I look to the side toward the cremation garden
where my father's ashes are not,
although a brass plaque bears his name:

Harvey—and his dates: 1918-2001.
His birthday an easy remembrance: *November 7, 1918,*
his death date fluid, moving target in my mind

I cannot keep fixed: Was it *April 24?*
I don't venture near the still garden
where other ashes mingle—and ours too, one day.

Ashes quiet beneath carpet of English ivy and
blanketed snow. I have his death certificate,
somewhere. Once settled at home,

I don't bother to look. Maybe it's
with the passports, the Social Security
cards and our baptismal records,

ashes to ashes, dust to dust.
Appropriately, my gardener father
is remembered in a cremation garden.

Annually I bare my forehead, priest pushes
fringe of bangs aside, says the words:
Remember you are dust, and to dust you shall return.

Marks me with a holy cross. I am
reminded of what I cannot change,
of what and of how precious is *this* day.

Day 2

Last year I gave up chocolate.
Ruined by Europeans: Swiss Lindor,
Belgian Côte d'Or and Guylian,

French Valhrona—Valhalla of chocolate.
The Côte d'Or I can't buy back home,
reserves from a trip to Provence long gone.

The inky black 100 Vigilucci I bought in Italy's Volterra,
a hilltown in Pisa County, granite black,
bitter, and dry, it played evil trickster to taste buds;

left them breathless. I invested half
of the Italian in a caramel cream tart,
elusive confection, set over medium heat;

left alone. Covered, ignored for
five unperturbed minutes
while patience is tested by sugar,

fresh lemon juice and water.
One cup of heavy double,
snow white cream sparks the action,
furiously whisked into the heaving mixture.

Steam, hiss and spit beneath my wooden spoon.
A task Herculean, monstrous battles,
impossibly re-imagined by

Hera to punish the hero,
and littered with hydras,
a gigantic crab…and Medusa.

I wonder how Caravaggio captured
her head—only her head,
gaping mouth open, defying death

and writhing snakes on a wooden shield,
tucked inside the Uffizi.
Dove Caravaggio—

I buy chocolate for home.
By New Year's it was gone.
Last year, I gave up chocolate for Lent.

This Lent is only beginning,
and I've decided against the letting go.

Day 5

The wild rabbit is gone.
Frenzied cat tracks interlaced
with soft padded impressions; snow remains

unblemished. Still, the rabbit
lived under the cedar deck on the south
side of my farmhouse, and he's gone.

I'd spotted him briefly sunning
and waiting, patiently like Ruth
and her secret evening gleaning times

in the golden wheat fields of Boaz.
So Boaz took Ruth and she was his wife:
In 1915, Grammy's marriage was so inscribed.

My rabbit sat, waited for wrens and starlings
to move along, waited to harvest cracked sunflower
husk and tender gray thistle from fevered repast.

Now he's gone, and I miss the vagrant
rabbit hobo in my yard. Taking up his post,
safe and sheltered under the deck

where I sun myself in early April.
As soon as the winds shift and chill softens
and sun's rays flex and stretch,

I steal a few quiet moments;
burnish myself on a mesh chaise
with coffee and a newspaper.

I've stopped placing a carrot atop new snow.
Since more cats showed up and it's Lent,
I withhold temptation.

Day 6

Pinocchio had no mother. I imagine
Gepetto carved the wooden boy
for company in the Tuscan hillside.

I grew up motherless, too;
never said goodbye.
My mother died alone.

In 1974, children were unwelcome
at hospital death bedsides. It remains
a dark hollow, I cannot fill.

Out of fierce love, we believe
we're protecting our children…
        —Dad, I don't blame you.

My young son tells me
he feels sorrow for me,
and I thank him for that.

Thank him for trying
to understand what
motherless means to me.

What I hide is how my sorrow
turns to terror at night
when my fist-sized heart soars

in flight and how I relive, re-imagine
her death all those years ago
every time I'm in a hospital, waiting.

How my wilderness stretches beyond
these 40 days, in every direction.

Day 8
February 24, 2010

Red roses wobble in a skinny vase
with curvaceous fluted edges. They sit at
table, upright, as if waiting

for breakfast to be served.
In the dining room a small bouquet
nests in a larger silver bowl,

its sheen reflects struggling sunlight,
as the tableau presses through
morning's somber, weighted clouds

swollen with tomorrow's snowstorm.
The roses are married off
to white Peruvian lily, *alstroemeria,*

glossy lemon leaves keep attendant company—
one rose for each of us.
Peruvian lily, opaque white and

embellished with butter yellow threads,
tiny yellow-tipped stamen nipples are
warm South American reminder of wealth.

These flowers feast
against a frugal landscape
and barren winter wilderness.

Prosperity and good fortune shrugged,
between flowers and lemon leaves.

Day 22

For birds in the garage,
I open doors. They find
their way to the side yard,

and freedom. Basement birds
are tougher. Frantic, they slam
into crumbling stone walls,

head for the light,
like dead souls after deciding
enough is enough,

cross the River Styx, leave
Caron bewildered with his ores
at the ready for a dignified crossing.

Like a bird, lighter than a whisper, the soul
must sense it no longer has to stumble around,
find a way to make a living, pay for dry cleaning

green grocer produce twice a week,
unscented laundry soap. It heads for illumination,
just like the starlings trapped in my darkened,

unfinished basement. The birds are startled
when they can't blast through plexiglass
mounted in rough hewn window wells .

Last summer a scrawny barn cat made her
new family in leftover maple leaves, damp and wet.
She nested and nursed younglings among English ivy.

Now the birds are desperate, desperate for safe passage,
for a clear line of sight to heaven.

Day 26

My son, Adam, stands freeze-framed.
His legs and arms ache in practiced position
feigning the upright cross bar.

He will portray Jesus on Good Friday,
depicting in a silent tableau
the scenes of the Passion of Christ.

It's a promotion. The past three years
he'd been a Centurion, shared lesser parts
in telling the annual Way of the Cross.

I will watch another child pretend whip my son.
A small Pontius Pilate will hold his hands,
suspended over a bowl filled with imagined water,

while yet another child as Roman guard stands
alongside with linen towel draped over his arm.
The weeping women will cover their faces.

I will watch two more diminutive soldiers,
bent over my son's pre-pubescent form, mallets
poised to hammer and tack his wrists to pretend wood.

I will share in some small, wrenching portion
of Mother Mary's heartbreak, her anguished
despair when they take His body down. Children will

wrap my son in a white shroud so thin—like breathing,
whispered kiss from head to foot, while
dimming lights distill the moment's grip.

Day 29

St. Patrick braved the clans and pagans,
used the pliant shamrock to explain Father,
Son and Holy Ghost to the mildly

curious, and to those he courted
for Christ's sake. St. Patrick's feast
marks a breaking of the fast

and a chance to dye fountains,
rivers and canals an unequivocal
shade of verdant green.

You can break
your Lenten fast
on St. Patrick's day, too.

Claim the Patron Saint of Ireland,
whether you protest or not,
are Catholic, or Irish, or not,

whether you even believe in anything,
besides a tepid glass of Guinness,
or Bushmills neat from the bottle; or not.

Day 32

Christ must have been tired, well into
the 40 wilderness days with nothing to eat.
Did He take fragrant water

from morning dews, cupped in leaves
or filling crevices or rocks, or
maybe He carried wineskin and

holy water replenishing, like the virgins
and their everlasting lamp oil.
Did He absently wander the desert

or know—just *know* which turns to take,
maybe He walked a colored mandala,
painstakingly pouring ochre

or cadmium colored sand from
small vials and once finished,
breathed out a moment in the sun,

sands swirled and patterns gone.
A thousand years, to God,
at least, is even like a day.

Maybe Jesus trailed His feet in the sand,
walked an unbroken circle in meditation
for 40 days, perhaps this is how

He passed the time. Was He flashpoint?
A speck to others squinting against horizon far?
Did He encounter scorpions, lizards

or the occasional oasis mirage
in haze of distance, ever out of reach.

Day 33

In some portions of the world,
there are those who choose to observe
the Way of the Cross.

They bear the sting of a lash.
They crawl on bloodied hands and knees
to a place where they are carefully crucified

to embrace a token bloodshed.
Just enough pain, just enough suffering,
just enough, to taste what Christ endured

among a teeming humanity.
Christ knew the grave was leveling field,
hillside and fresh hewn cave could not bind.

How brave will I be at the moment I face death.
Christ knew the emptiness of darkened sepulcher,
knew it was transition, from His humanity

to the place He shed the need for skin,
coursing blood, hunger and thirst,
wakefulness; sleep.

All this to join again, partake again,
of the divine without the need for breath.
He left behind friends, family—mother,

the devoted. Those who believed; those who didn't.
His transcendence not hammering fist but
palm outstretched; a place to touch, an open offering.

Lazarus

My name cried out,
resounding across the desert,

filtering through the veins
of tomb and rock, scored

and snugly fitted against
smooth, alabaster stone.

I am standing up, moving
within the tired cloth

strips of burial clothing
fragrant with myrrh; with sadness.

Flesh knits together.
Scabs fall away.

I am called out into
the butterscotch sun.

Heart and lungs begin, in concert.
I feel it all.

The linen napkin draped slack,
slants across my jaw, open once more.

Day 38

I would have red onions sown by now,
and 10 pounds of Yukon gold potatoes
safety tucked into long rows

marked by clay pots and
tamped down on the ends of the lines.
I'd be buying seeds.

Lemon and Teddy bear sunflowers.
Cut and Come Again zinnias and
Mesclun mix—sweet and bitter salad greens.

Not this year. I don't even have
pansies yet, their perky faces upturned to
eastern rising sun, usually clustered in an urn

by the French doors at the back.
This year my garden will lie fallow.
When the soil warms and the February

snow pack and residue of early March rain
siphons away from the Black eyed Susans
and False Indigo, I'll cautiously test the

ground for weight before I enter its gate.
This year is restoration.
Tons of topsoil to be hauled

and shoveled into the dips, gullies and
trenches years of planting, growth
and harvest have made.

I'll empty my compost pile, and
till the rich loam, wriggling with earthworms
into newborn soil.

Earthworms, the size of young garter snakes,
will hold court. Honeybees knowingly whisper
to bergamot, *next year, oh yes, next year.*

Day 41

I look for brown Mission figs
at the nearby farmers market,
check the fruit lodged in green

woven baskets for nicks, for skin
bruises, I take one to breathe deep
the muddy Turkish soil.

Maybe Jesus cursed the fig tree
because He was hungry, after all, branches
empty, nothing worthwhile to offer or receive.

Fresh figs are a treat in late winter.
I can imagine why Jesus, having walked for miles
with dust needling skin beneath sandals,

the scent of wearied days filling his head,
would have hungered for a rich, fresh
fig from the source. How He

might have become disgusted
by the tree's bad timing. Jesus
had healed the sick, raised the dead,

was on His own path to death. Were
the disciples alarmed as an unfamiliar
knife edge sharpened their master's voice?

Perhaps His empty wine skin
or water jug was pronounced
a kinder, gentler judgment.

These vessels dodged the curse,
and the fig tree, blinded, was
unable to escape His wrath.

Day 45

In one scene, during
The Way of the Cross,
my son, Adam, hangs his head

before the boy playing Pontius
Pilate and the children dressed
as guards flanking the tableau.

In another moment, the guards and soldiers
suspend their arms, fingers clenched
around imaginary dice, to see

whose gamble wins the cloak.
Adam stands off to the side, draped
in white and stripped of everything.

Veronica kneels frozen, as Adam falls
for the third time on the journey to Calvary.
She wipes the sweat from his forehead

with a white handkerchief.
Another child—Adam's friend since the
nursery, plays Joseph of Arimathea,

cradles Adam's head in her lap.
Christ was released in death from the cross.
Sometimes I don't see it's the need

to forgive holding me back.
Not confrontation of an angry other,
who may offer contempt of a pure

gift offering forgiveness yields.
Even if the words—*I forgive you*—are said alone,
out loud; more for my own redemption.

The Great Vigil

Adam asks what happened to Jesus
between the crucifixion and Easter Sunday.
We call it Holy Saturday—the day of waiting.

Jacob wrestled with God,
through the sweat-stained night
until dawn's first threaded light.

Jacob refused to let go until
Jehovah blessed him, offered him
a sign, a seal of protection—forever.

Jesus cast seven demons from
Mary Magdalene. He sent Legion away
from the demon possessed, innumerable,

and the demons fled the two young men,
entered the swine herd. Torn and
crazed, they rushed the cliff.

The boy who was possessed, too, bashed
and hurled himself against the rocks—
he was freed of affliction.

Once again the boy could look into
his father's face with adoring eyes.
On the day of waiting,

Jesus must have looked straight at Lucifer,
stared him square in the eye.

Day 60

I've been looking for you
since Easter and the resurrection.
Looking for moments

when you appeared
to those who loved you:
Mary at the tomb, the disciples

locked up, hidden away in their anguished
terror in the room where you'd
washed their feet; shared a meal.

It's hard to see, *to really see* miracles now,
away from the Jerusalem you knew,
but I'm trying. I'm digging deep, for

the moments you were with your own:
on the beach making fish breakfast,
loading once empty fishing nets, recast to

overflow, because you said so.
Peter jumped into the water
fully clothed, to reach you.

There were more appearances.
Still, I can't help but wonder
what you did when you were alone,

without an audience. Where were you during
those 50 days until Pentecost's fire and tongues?

Every apple was a seed

Gala, Empire, Red and Yellow Delicious,
Esopus Spitzenburg, Winesap, Northern Spy.
Their stories began in the moist earth,
and Gaia looks after her children.

Enough sunshine and rain softens brittle
outer hull, causes pulp to swell and burst
its casement. I am trucking in topsoil
to shore up my plot, fill scoops and troughs.

I tell my son, *no vegetables this year,*
while we make ready for years to come.
Unsatisfied, he pleads, wheedles,
cajoles, speaks in glowing young words of

harvest, of burnished pumpkins, deeply ribbed,
of sunflower heads and porch decoration.
My resolve begins to fracture, to open,
just a little, then open up some more,

until I am buying *Big Max* and *Ghost Rider* seed
to sow, tend and harvest for Jack-O-Lanterns
in October. We agree, strike a bargained compromise:
I ensure enough ground is made ready.

For his part, he will help me tend
fallow soil, put the whole in balance.

Day 77

One cousin tells me lightly
her ashes will become fish food,
floating across the surface

of the Pacific Ocean, off the
San Francisco harbor before
becoming weighted down

with salt and sea water.
Another cousin begins
and ends her day with prayer.

She holds a focused doctrine,
based on literal and immutable
translations of God's word.

Translations by men she can accept
and take into herself, without question.
As for me, faith tenders all hope.

It binds divine promises:
holds fast without letting go.

Day 82

Praying's the cheapest, first-rate medicine I know,
said Burt Lancaster in *Elmer Gantry* (United Artists, 1960)

My son saves his prayers for bedtime,
singsong chants the *Our Father,* and
Now I Lay Me Down to Sleep.

At twelve, he doesn't leave out the part
about dying before he wakes,
the plea for God to take his soul.

Sometimes I hear his supplications
long after he should be dreaming.
On school nights I say, *go to sleep.*

I know he won't be content until
his list is exhausted, touches each
name with his voice, sends an urgent call

for aging family members. Comfort
and grace when Aunt Shirley was dying,
for Uncle Clem's soul after his death.

I listen to his prepubescent voice,
high enough to mirror the tone
and timber of a younger child.

Although he is already showing signs,
his manhood beginning. Soft hair grows
longer underneath his arms,

blond leg and arm hair knits a little thicker:
Still, his voice remains the same.
His vocal chords are thin,

like upper register strings on a lute,
high clean notes release
his faithfulness to heaven.

Day 84

In the beginning was the word.
The darkness cried out for a word,
and the light suffered in silence

until illumination was named.
We name children, call ourselves wife,
husband, daughter, son, father, mother

brother, niece, nephew, friend, or enemy.
We name our nationality, contain our
borders by rivers, mountains or lakes,

name those, too. This is New Jersey and this,
Pennsylvania. We contain by language,
skirt what language allows to loosen.

Nimrod, great-grandson of Noah
and the flood, aspired to become like God.
He wanted to touch the heavens,

like God reaches out to Adam
with one fingertip poised, Nimrod, too,
would breathe the breath of God.

He ordered bricks to be made, and tar
to seal the bricks, and Babel was shattered
before it was. Language cursed,

scattered and littered. When the
Holy Spirit came, and Christ made Ascension,
again there was speaking in tongues

of flame and joy. Words filled each mouth, each
syllable a morsel to savor, to name; swallow.

Moments and Consequence

I take the offered gift, stop and sit
in one of two café chairs
placed at a stone table out back.

Most days, I push these fleeing thoughts
and few precious moments aside.
My day's intentions honest,

and these moments brushed off,
filled with *afters:* Breakfast dishes,
wet shirts or underwear hung out on the line.

Start a cake to baking. Chop pecans for sticky buns.
Run the vacuum cleaner. Dust.
Tidy rooms when *I* am untidy.

Most mornings I begin with work.
Settle in for an early hour or two,
push aside the pull of blue sky, of

clean, fragrant north winds and
no cow smell, no barn smell, no
whiff of moldering hay.

No, none of these today, when
wind is gentle and resolved, like
my toddler's grip and tug on skirt's hem,

like my young son, this breeze too insistent to resist.

III

Artichoke—a thistle, the globe or French
artichoke consumed before buds bloom

Winter Morning, 6AM

after Charles Simic Summer Morning

I know all the dark places
the sun hasn't touched:
My toes buried beneath flannel sheets,

the dog's food dish,
fracture tracing the lilac's reflection
on the north side of the farmhouse.

Wren risks affliction for seed
at the base of the yearling maple.
She is both hesitant and resilient

amid a throng of boisterous chickadees.
A pair of cardinals are bent
on making war in the distance.

Along the frozen tractor ruts,
silent skating ponds in the wheat field,
a petulant stone cracks.

Sleeping spiders store next year's lingerie
deep inside their unmoving bellies. Firewood whispers,
cautions cast from last night's storm.

I stretch out my limbs, arms and legs together
wiggle toes, before slipping out of bed.
Lately I've been shoving my feet

inside my slippers, I never used to.
Preferring to cushion my heels
against slope of pumpkin pine flooring.

I purpose my spine, set my chin
defiant against early morning chill,
make ready to step into this new day.

Chez le Charcuterie

For Lou Passante—Menerbes, 2004

The butcher shop features local
specialties, tight in the center of a knot
of stone and clay roof houses.

Streets lacing Menerbes,
a medieval hilltop village,
carved out of quiet rock.

Lou steps out of a back room. His
nose, jaw line, and forehead are sharply
angled like blades on his meat cutters.

The back room shielded
by long strings of amber beads,
nod to America's Woodstock.

I want the lamb chops.
I order two in French.
I want the sopressata, too,

and thick, glistening sausages.
joined by a single thread.
He warms to me.

We pore over my translation dictionary.
Chat. He is kind, nods; becomes
flirtatious, asks where I'm from,

New York, he questions with glinting eyes,
I say, no, Philadelphia.
A knowing look spreads

across his face. *Philadelphie*
he repeats, as if the expanse
of the United States

can be boiled down
like water to poach fish,
into one east coast city.

I am convinced in another
10 minutes he'd invite me
through the amber glass beads.

Motion with his seasoned hands, pull back
the threads stretching to the tile floor into
sanctuary and spice of a butcher's back room.

L'Isle sur la Sorgue
Provence April, 2004

There is a small church
at the base of town, and
a few Euro clicks on the lights.

Windows are tiny squares. Prayer tables
stocked with votives for the faithful.
We light candles for our dead.

It is said the dusky smoke
from the quickened flame
carries prayer to heaven.

A small stand sells sugar crepes,
at a truck pizza by the slice.
Lights rim bare awning frames

and empty cafés line the walkway.
The gray mouth of Fountaine-de-Vaucluse
shudders out of the mountain,

feeds the river Sorgue.
Divers descend to 1,000 meters and
still fail to fingertip the bottom.

The water's sensuous slide
whispers pleasure, splits to surround
the town, quick-step to rushing water.

It percolates from deep inside
the mountain, slips over rocks,
tumbles algae fingers along the runway.

At the mouth of the cave mist from the river
showers through cleaving boulders, washing us.

D'accord!

D'accord to the chemist,
and halting directions from his shop
to warm croissants and patisserie tucked

behind the village butchers, like
a wisp of silken hair to the ear.
D'accord to Provencal pizza,

earthen black olive, epicenter,
to lunch slices devoured
in an outdoor St. Remy café,

scant blocks from van Gogh's pain.
The Dutchman inside his vintner's
cave tosses back his head,

serves up house vintage, curled expanse
of grapes and tangled vines sprawled,
testing for a toe hold at the foot

of the Luberon mountains.
His laugh is round and full,
a cabaret song, as he pours our wine.

Behind the counter stained casks,
color of midnight back home,
sit settled behind the counter.

To the rented house in Menerbes,
d'accord and *oui*—as we pull away
from stones culled at Cassis,

rocky landscape touching Mediterranean sea.
My young son, Adam arranged his stones
on the mantel, slyly slipped a few

into his pockets against my warnings
they belong in France, at home, I caution.
Adam waves to the house, while his treasure

sits in silence inside the rental house,
tears rimming his clear blue eyes.

Menerbes France, 2004

I thread my way into town, buy our daily
baguette, freshly baked and madeleines
dusted white, airy and orange scented.

Since the Phoenicians claimed Marseille,
mingled blood, marriage and bouillabaisse
we drove to Cassis instead, took the tour

out into the sea. The boat moves in cascade dips,
spearhead swells as salt and sea and
wind whips French children's frightened

tears from their eyes, to ours.

Le Baux a mighty castle fortress,
Gordes dry stone bories hut communes
stand tall for a thousand years or more.

Olive groves tumble down the mountain,
the man and his wife push a wheelbarrow loaded,
heavy with weeds and olive branch trimmings.

Nearby, another local burns discarded
branches, scent of crying olives drifting up.
In Menerbes the vineyard's lazy stretch

across the valley and distance to Alpine borders is vast, content.

Once home, I cut fabric from the Cavaillon market—
a bargain of patterns I'd find nowhere else.
At nine Euro a metre, I buy five.

Hung over from jet-lag, I fashion pillows
with fringe and pre-formed fill, these local
trimmings now married to French fabric forever.

Driven to finish these gifts, I realize
one hundred meters of such cloth would
not be enough. I vow to return

to buy more fabric; hone my French.

On That Day

*'Marie Clotide' tells of the day before her Queen's death,
Marie Antoinette's court (1755-1820)*

Chicken consommé, wild morels,
a fist of shallots, handful of chives:
these comprised her final meal.

I made Marie Antoinette's soup, though
I am no cook. Sliced the pleated
morel caps, tops like a generous penis.

Shallots I cut razor thin. Turned the softened
sauté into the stock, tipped rough brandy into the pan,
secret hidden treasure strapped to my thigh.

There was no gateau, no chevré,
no bouillabaisse laden with prawns, oysters,
hake and savory, steaming broth.

No sweet cream, no chocolate,
no dainties offered up—
no strawberries to kiss

at picnics on the lawn of Versailles
strewn with wandering peacocks.
No Chenin Blanc, no Chardonnay.

Our tears dried up,
their wellspring bone dry.
Let them eat cake was farce,

cruel concoction, whispered plot to poison
her people against Marie Antoinette.
False words trotted out against other

French Queens in other times, too.
I fastened the white corset for the last time,
true color of mourning for the Queens of France.

I trussed her bosom and heart together.
Hold tight, I whispered to clothing
binding her, hook and eye,

clasps clenched, *hold fast, hold true.*

The Artichokes
Provence France, 2004

I consider the artichokes in Bonnieux,
clustered in a wooden crate beside
fingerling potatoes and stout field carrots.

These are backed up against the stone wall,
and market square, a hand-cut plateau
from the grooved, vineyard valley and rows below.

Buckets of lavender, cached
Lily of the Valley, *Muguet,*
a Coty scent my grandmother

would dab on handkerchiefs trimmed
with own her hand-made fragile lace,
tucked into apron pockets.

I found the handkerchiefs when she died.

Scarlet poppies in cloistered bunches,
local wine at 9 a.m., fresh goat chevré
dusted with cracked pepper. Mussels.

Fat crabs, and thick sea fillets
all hunkered down on beds of crushed ice.
At 10 a.m., a man lights a flame

chickens roasting on tall shelving racks,
tall, slim and bronzed - like the Provencal people.
Chickens turn on spits above gas flames.

I am tempted to buy a bottle
of white wine and settle on gray stone wall
with a roasted chicken in my lap.

The artichokes intrigue. Coy, huddled together,
perhaps murmuring about their futures,
from stories passed down, or passing shopper's

gossip about meal-making, about steaming in pots
service with cheese, or appetizer to fish,
arranged on a narrow wooden dining table

in an amber soup tureen, dressed up
with coarse breadcrumb. I skip
the artichokes—*I buy them canned at home*—

and imagine the fisted leaves yielding
to tickling water boiling at the rental house.
The slide of tongue and scrape of teeth

critical to conquer the tough thistle skin.
I buy strawberries instead—safe, easy and
some mixed field greens laced with endive.

I buy chocolate. Thick hunks of Savon
de Marseille soup, rosé from Cassis and linens:
Provencal linens, to remind me.

View Near Volterra I

—Ascending the highest point in Tuscany
by Jean Baptiste Camille Corot

Volterra's road winds sharp,
unforgiving, razer ribbon
and tightly wound corkscrew

up and up, threading to
open expanses of road below.
I wonder how many

breathless steps Corot took,
along with his faithful mule,
and carrying what?

Clay for local potters in bargain?
Canvas? Oils? Palette knife and brushes,
mineral spirits for cleaning, turpentine?

Did he linger in mountain's cleft,
in veins of all kinds, seek a place, an opening?
Corot could not have known this.

His pastoral scene, lush and idyllic,
as if green would be, could be, anything
more than landscape, among

the thousands of other landscapes
of Tuscan hilltowns. We journeyed
on an Italian bus headed

for ancient cobblestone square,
clock tower, kitschy tourist shops,
espresso, gelato, chocolate so dark

it landed dry on the tongue.
The Etruscan Museum where
pre-Roman remains lay enshrined,

mute in funerary vessels crafted
from hillside alabaster, also hidden.
Thousands of years, keeping silence.

Abraham's Knife

I have been holstered like this before.
The old man carefully wiped me with lambskin,
dressed me again, stropped from hilt to vertex

with raw, bristling wool. I know sacrifice.
He loads the gentle ass with
thin-skinned cypress sticks.

He calls the boy, *Isaac,*
who comes, throws himself
into the waiting arms of the father.

"Were do we travel today?"
the expectant, radiant child questions.
Not far, Abraham answers,

his name recast from
Abram, a distinction proffered
like a crown of rubies, of emeralds.

He is become the father of Israel.
God promised descendents
surpassing even grains of sand

spanning the continents; the world.
Isaac runs ahead, joyous to be
with Father, as I slap the old man's thigh.

Gently we climb rocks,
kick up dust—my shine dulled,
all head into the division.

There is no goat, no lamb.
The Lord will provide,
Abraham tells himself out loud,

as much as he speaks to Isaac,
who turns and skips ahead
as unaware as I, of the coming.

I shiver, sensing ground and trembling
as Abraham palms my hilt.
The boy, terrified, remains obedient—

obedient unto death. Isaac lay
splayed across the alter rock.
God stays my master's grip

sends a lamb into the clearing.
Satisfied, the lamb's blood soaks me,
teardrops from my point.

Hallelujah. Hallelujah. Hallelujah.

The man who was beaten and robbed
—Luke's account of The Good Samaritan, The Bible, New Testament

I was headed to Jericho,
unsure of the way, I had not
journeyed this road before.

Amid the silence and desert,
I heard cushioned footfalls behind me.
This should have been a sign.

I felt a sharp blade pressed
against my neck, hairs along my nape
rose up, my breath hostage in my throat.

The stink of rotting teeth marked my jaw.
Later, I woke naked. Grit settled in my mouth.
Someone was bending over me,

covering me with a blanket,
draped me over a donkey,
the familiar comfort of animal scent.

I don't know where this new man came from.
His smell leather and chickpeas.
From my swollen eyes, I barely see his face.

I don't know where he is taking me…it almost doesn't matter.

My House

He's building a handrail
in the basement, to steady
the rickety stairs. I want

to write a poem about my house.
Not the one we pay the mortgage
to keep, or its stewardship of 200 years;

us in the thick of it.
Or basement waters from rain,
loose stone foundation,

how it pinions everything.
My house, a gray Atlas of pebbles,
shoring up dry oak beams,

clay brick and stucco skins,
my world poised, shouldered.
No, I've written about that house

before. I want to write
about my dwelling place.
Where I am wrapped in skin, built

from miraculous muscle, tendon,
from bone. I want to write about
torn cartilage, about surgery,

about how my recovery continues,
because I'm not fixed yet.
I want to go deeper.

The surgeon shows me the wonder
on a digitized screen, the work
his hands have wrought.

His masterpiece, sculpted
from my clumsy, raw clay.
My cartilage malformed

in my mother's womb.
How this surgeon changed it.
How he changed the shape

of everything, and I must learn
to walk again. Of how I refused
to cut my hair since the surgery—

like my strength comes from it.

Lot's Wife

after Wistawa Szymborska

I had been warned.
Did I swirl, a salt dervish
of my own accord,

atoms strewn and cast to plain winds?
Or stand as pillar of salt suddenly priceless,
highly prized, ancient world currency,
now trenched into the already writhing soil.

I would not have wanted it this way. Perhaps
I was anxious, as we gathered up our
few things, frantically searching for precious items:

My silver bowl, a missing
sandal, its mate hastily tied
around slender ankle,

clay storage vessels for flour and wheat.
A wine skin for the journey ahead.
My house in disarray.

Lot searching for our daughters' husbands.
Lot checking the goats. Lot wondering
where he'd left the oil and lamps.

We left the chickens behind,
flapping and clucking in panic,
their eyes popping, feathers useless

against God's rage.
Then I heard the sound
of anguished screaming,

or was it mocking laughter?
A moment later, the hollow
sound of silence.

I can't say why
I looked back.
Habit really.

Perhaps I looked back
after setting my bundle
down to stretch.

Perhaps I looked back,
absently pushing a strand
of hair from my face.

I looked back, toward Sodom,
and then I looked no more.

The heart is a moving target

Clutched between ribs, held up
by supporting muscles, sinew, veins
and arteries and cased within

a chest wall wrapped in skin, it moves
when I move. It washes the car,
cooks Belgian waffles, reads

bedtime stories. Types. Flutters
and flumps, quickens and
skips the odd, occasioned beat.

Other times I feel the scattered, hesitant thud
while bending from the waist to retrieve
a log from the firewood stack, a missed beat

as I fall asleep on my right side—never the left,
or when I hold onto a moment's breath
during early morning love making.

Walking might jar the heart, its rhythmic stride
calming some terrified self-protection.
My cardiologist tells me the heart moves

when we move. It doesn't sit still in womb-like
suspended animation, or work
its will alone. No. It works in concert

with organs, coursing blood collapse
and expansion of lungs. Hard pressed,
embraced by a loved one; rent in two.

It never sleeps—its dependable squeeze and release.

Preferences

after Wistawa Szymborska

I prefer red.
Dangly earrings to studs,

summer to winter, twilight's hush
to dawn, sunset to sunrise.

I prefer the slick silence of varnished oak
to the hushed breath of bare wood.

Lamb to pork and ribs to roasts - except Prime Rib,
which is both rib and roast. I prefer chardonnay

to all other white wines. I prefer pinot noir, and
Royal Bitch shiraz. I prefer pears. Blackberries

to raspberries, except in Kir Royale.
I prefer tree gnarls to smooth trunks,

and limbs with bird feeders hanging from them.
I prefer bird song to begin the day, and as call

to suppertime. I prefer laughter and alto voices,
Charles Wesley hymns to Martin Luther's.

I prefer chocolate. Period.
I prefer periods to bossy exclamation points,

and I prefer questions to all other punctuation,
except when I prefer commas, used sparingly.

I prefer to be able to prefer, except
when preferences are discarded, or unavailable.

Then I prefer to be finished.

Alphabet 2

I hold the Phoenicians responsible,
even though it was really the Romans
who get all the credit for the alphabet's creation.

The Phoenicians loaded the sea with boats,
subdued, wooed then married Gaul, Sicily,
Spain, Morocco and bouillabaisse.

Today I am making bouillabaisse,
substitute Chilean Sea bass for hake fillets
I can't find at home.

Was it like that, use what you've got at hand,
when Jesus fed the 5,000 on the mountainside?
What variety of fish was served that day?

And the rolls—were they crusty like sourdough
or hard, worn and seaworthy, something
you could sop into hasty fisherman's stew.

In a skilled cook's capable hands, bouillabaisse
consists of crustacean's, firm fin fish, onions, leeks,
saffron, orange peel, tomatoes and garlic—a wondrous broth.

It is a sea unto itself in a bowl.
A steaming marvel ladled into a tureen,
flaky pastry puffed, perched on top.

Was it happy accident or purpose, that brought
the Phoenicians to Cassis, moon cresting
into tourmaline Mediterranean Sea?

In tribute to Chez Vincent's, the
Phoenicians, Cassis and my bouillabaisse
a toast: my glass raised high.

Wintering Bluebirds

I spotted them weeks ago, an accident.
Flush of orange belly against a gray morning sky,
vibrant blue head, back and wings.

The birds attracted by Christmas greens,
now past their prime in Epiphany,
arranged in urns by my back door.

Winterberries nestled with care
into these arrangements,
their plump ruby morsels

cling to woody stems.
Relentless pair of Eastern bluebirds
settle on my red maple's

bare branches; they linger.
The adolescent maple is replacement
for an old warrior whose time

had come and gone.
My winterberries are running out.
I head to the local nursery yard,

knock hard on the house door. Wait.
Through the window a warm,
noisy, messy kitchen. The closed sign

hangs sad, and askew.
The yard is barren, wearing
winter's dark overcoat.

Christmas trees once upright,
fluffed out, boughs fragrant
with pine oil lay flat; abandoned.

I knock on the house door,
ask to buy more winterberry.
He tells me *no,*

just cut what you want, take it.
He pauses, *leave some,*
we have bluebirds, too.

He tells me this before closing the door.
I pull on gloves, palm pruners,
walk to the back and a standing

trinity of winterberry bushes.
All in a row, they struggle
against an alternately cruel

and indifferent midwinter.
I bring fresh cuttings home. Mild recent
days have made soil moist, pliant.

I jab the fresh winterberry branches deep,
next to empty twigs stripped clean of harvest.
I whisper a prayer to the bluebirds: Stay.

Dreamscape

I am driving in the dream. I know these country roads
with names like Old Bethlehem, California,
and East Pumping Station. In my gray-scaled vision,

the roads are nuanced. Sudden water floods them,
although there is no rain—has been no rain for days.
Frightened I want to turn back, turn my black car

around, refuse the water pushing toward me
like walking upstream against crush of crowded
streets in Philadelphia. There are other cars,

other drivers cast in silhouette.
Could these drivers be dreaming, too?
As if by some common thread we tapped

the same dreamscape at the same time,
and all chose to drive the same cars
otherwise parked safely, tucked into garages

or in claimed spaces in front of homes.
Why did we make the choice to navigate
unfamiliar, brackish water together, and apart?

Some of the drivers cut the surface, sluicing through
shallows, creating sharkfin flows
all the while the water refills, becomes deeper,

almost sinister, more treacherous to traverse.

Wood and Yield

For Phil

He can tell you the name of a tree
by its bark—rough, curled or smooth
to palm or fingertip,

by translucent emerging leaves in May,
vein maps running life force
like the back of a hand.

The rust or amber of fall foliage,
scent and trail of sap. Injuries sustained—
how a tree will heal itself, scab, scar or

if the wound is fatal. He knows their canvas hues.
Darkening green comes in August, September's
first flutter and drop times. Which grain lengths

are easily sliced, like an orange or hammered
hard like ironwood—yes, it lives up
to its name. At his age, he avoids mulberry's greedy grit.

My husband knows wood, the way he knows me.
Knows the overnight dependable burn of
red and white oak—these he prizes.

He understands the fickle youth of birch, poplar,
Bradford pear. How they cycle briefly, like
new flame: Seed to branch; woodstove to ash.

With a smile he can coax glowing coals
forth from grayed cinders, seeming spent.

Paradise Found

This winter was hard on the dwarf pines,
their needles brittle, stems tough, sullen, brown.

Six months later pliant green shoots wave gently in mid-air.
Bigger pots promise a roomy housing upgrade.

Time to grow. Time for roots to stretch, and drink deep.
Next comes color, planters filled to overflow.

Lime colored trailing vinca rimmed with white,
proud dracaena spike for height.

I like it crowded. Vivacious orange Nonstop begonias,
their petals unfurling like rejoicing cabbage roses.

Purple Wave petunias for cascade. Alluring Red Hot Poker salvia
bows slightly, flutters and winks in light breezes.

There's a table for two, and I sit alone.
Like a lizard I bask in early June sunshine,

content in my corner of paradise found.

Pie Making

I'd watch you peeling fresh white peaches,
wiping a forearm on cotton apron,
and whittling the skin, one by one,

from each piece of fragrant fruit.
I am no longer twelve
recently made motherless,

and learning in a dark adolescent kitchen
the wonders from you of pie making.
Mixing pastry without measurements

scratching in the lard with white flour
adding drops of water from a dented tin cup.
Feel it, you'd say to me, *with both hands.*

And after ingredients were bound
into a pat-ball, you'd scrape fingers
and palms with the dull back of a dinner knife,

your hands would be the final test.
I imagine those hands,
paper thin and gently brushing

my son's delicious, infant skin, buttery;
soft, like rich sweet pastry. Adam is nearly
12, and I am teaching him

to mix pastry without measurements.
Scatter ice water over flour and butter crumbs
like sowing rye grass seed.

To feel it ready for rolling, *feel it,*
as you once told me, with both hands.

Gardener's Gift

There will be more.
White wine to deglaze the pan as
onion slices sizzle and caramelize.

Reincarnated over and over, mild or sharp
onions pulled from the warm earth,
paper skins allowed to cure in the sun

on a carpet of moist grass.
The raw pieces, splintered
with measured strokes of a sharp knife.

An onion, one ingredient measured out
piquant spark in autumn soup, taste of sunshine,
swathed with thick slices of Gruyere

and mixed with beef bone broth, a French homage.
It's all for the best. Scraps and kitchen cleanings
transformed by fat earthworms

in my compost pile behind the woodshed.
The cycle begins anew as I haul top dressing
out to the drowsy garden from groggy bin,

gardener's rich, intentional brandy.
Plant food turned over with sleepy soil in spring.
It's not a bad deal, after all.

About the Author

Melinda Rizzo wrote her first poem when she was about five years old. She's been writing poetry ever since that bright yellow, No. 2 pencil scribble—acknowledged as real art by her mother.

A freelance reporter and writer by trade, she believes poetry informs her non-fiction work, which circles back to feed her poetry.

Her media and publishing career of more than 30 years began with typesetting seed catalogs at W. Atlee Burpee. It continued with producing first printing self-help, craft, cooking and gardening books at the former Rodale Press in Emmaus. It continues with reporting news and features for B2B, local and regional publications. She also works to further the mission of Upper Bucks Chamber of Commerce in Quakertown, Pennsylvania, through their online blog, various content, and annual membership directory and community profile.

While digital content reigns and not one of us knows where the next information revolution will lead, there is nothing, *nothing,* like ink on paper. For authentic escape, growth and learning the look, feel and discovery found by turning the pages of a book is nonpareil.

Melinda shares a 200-year-old farmhouse, writes, bakes, cooks and gardens in rural Upper Bucks County, Pennsylvania, with her childhood sweetheart and husband Phil, their young adult son Adam, and a fine succession of English Labrador retrievers—the best dogs in this universe, or any other!!

Made in the USA
Monee, IL
22 February 2020